To: Brenda

♡ Sandy

MERRY CHRISTMAS JACKASS!

Sandy Thornton

DEDICATION:

This book is for all of my fellow "beepers."

My granddaughter, Madelyn, coined the term "beeper," referring to the sound an item makes as it is scanned at the point of sale.

If you have ever been behind a cash register, my friend, then this book is for you.

Merry Christmas!

STOP PAYING WITH EXACT CHANGE

If the total of your purchase is $12.56 and you hand over $22.06, you are just hurting everyone.

Usually, people say, "Does this help?"

... Help whom?

It isn't helping the four people waiting behind you, while you dig in that hobo knapsack of yours. Why is all of your change spilled in the bottom of your purse? With gas receipts and gum from 2009?

The next time you sit down to watch Chicago Fire, get yourself a big black lawn-sized trash bag and organize your purse, for God's sake! Have some self-respect.

"Sorry. My purse is so heavy. I need to get rid of some change."

You are carrying around half of your worldly possessions.

Pretty sure it isn't the change, Sis.

What does your car look like?

You have three wallets and some sort of accordion file filled with expired coupons. You are not fooling anyone. You have never saved $1, and even if you had...you could not find it.

Be an organized jackass, for the love.

LOCKED DOORS

When a door is locked, pulling on the handle repeatedly will not disengage the mechanism.

Because....Well, science. "Open at 10:00am," **in fact**, means 10:00am.

Frowning at the sign and looking in, in a hostile manner, does not alter that fact.

Yelling, "I only need one thing!" is not a compelling argument. There is no money in the till, the lights are off, and I am still brushing my teeth.

10:00am.

A counter argument would be to yell, "I only need 47 things!" That might be worth opening the door for.

Also, we prefer to lock the door at closing and return to our homes and families.

Don't rush in 2 minutes prior to closing saying that you only need one thing!

This is usually partnered with, "I know you are ready to go home!"

DO you know that? It seems as if you do NOT know that. I promise you that no matter what is happening at home — house fire, ugly divorce, an ill child with vomiting and diarrhea —all of it is preferable to work. GET OUT.

We literally hate you, you jackass.

WHITE MAN JOKES

Stop making stupid jokes at the cash wrap. The cashier is not married to you, or in a relationship with you, and therefore should not have to hear it.

The old "Does this come in MY size?" or "There is no tag, it must be free!" is tired.

Exhausted, really.

My personal favorite: When I request a phone number for the rewards program...

"Wow! I am a married man! My wife won't like that! Maybe buy me dinner first."

Har.De.Har.Har....Your wife doesn't even want your phone number. Trust. Me.

Just quietly pay and walk out to your Ford F150 for the love of God.

When my husband tried to do this (years before he had been through training), I whispered "STOP." They hate you.

He learned. That is what we call "coaching in the moment" or "delivering difficult feedback."

Sometimes he can't help himself and I get it. It is just part of being a white man. It is involuntary.

Like a burp.

P.S. I can't NOT attack middle-aged to elderly white women. The absolute meanest demographic in America. Manicured hands down. Queens of the jackasses.

CELL PHONE COURTESY

Sharing means caring — except when it applies to your private phone conversations.

Please do not carry your phone around on speaker.

My mom watched **The Days of Our Lives** when I was growing up. I have five children. I have heard enough drama for a lifetime. My platter is full.

Your advice to your cousin regarding her relationship is going unheeded. **Trust me.** I assure you, it is.

Once, I heard a two-sided conversation between a woman and a nurse regarding a colonoscopy.

Graphic details. Details about the symptoms leading up to the procedure, the procedure itself, and the brutal aftermath.

(Stephen King would have vomited.)

It is just too much for an hourly employee to have to hear.

When approaching the cash wrap, please end your call. We are trying to capture every single detail about you and your life in hope that we can get you to come back in and spend your last $8.

Pay attention. Give information freely and enunciate.

Your cousin's relationship issue will still be there when you get in your car. Your cousin is a wreck, admit it. Just don't share it with us at the register. We don't care.

Your cousin is also a jackass.

"Well, they can't all be winners."

Bad Santa

SUPPLY AND DEMAND

Sometimes in life we want to buy things that are not available for purchase.

There are many reasons for this. Maybe other people are also interested in purchasing this item and when we reach the store it is no longer available. Maybe there was a global pandemic, and the entire world is experiencing shipping and receiving issues.

It happens.

Yes, it can be upsetting.

I would like to mention, however, that Christmas does fall on the same day each year. We are all aware that it is coming. And when.

It is not a surprise, like, say..... a global pandemic.

We can prepare for Christmas and this keeps us from losing our tempers, yelling, cussing, crying, and blaming others for our lack of foresight.

This keeps us from crying and pounding on locked doors while yelling "I ONLY NEED ONE THING!"

This keeps employees from walking to On the Border in the Wichita Falls, Texas mall and having shots in the bar on their lunch break. (Not me. I was picking up enchiladas. I drown my stress and sorrow in cheese.)

So, let's all agree to breathe and shop early! Be planful.

Be kind to the service industry employees that are just trying to survive each day.

Let's not punish them for our shortcomings.

Or late goings, you jackass.

ECOMM

Brick and mortar: On the way to becoming extinct.

How do we compete? How do we save these old school dinosaurs and compete with Amazon? You got me.

Amazon RULES.

RULES.

My husband and I were discussing "cancel culture" and Amazon was mentioned.

I told him if Jeff Bezos started crucifying people in the streets, I would not cancel my Prime membership.

Uh uh. Nope.

So in a desperate attempt to stay relevant and compete, companies are offering **BOPIS.**

Buy Online and Pick Up in Store.

The teeny, tiny, little problem with **BOPIS** is that it relies on correct inventory information. Unfortunately, it is not an exact science. Sometimes the website will say an item is in stock, when it is, in fact, not in stock. Those of us in the field love **BOPIS.**

It adds a fun new element to our already miserable existence.

You order it and pay for it but we do not actually have it.

You call and have a fit.

You come in and have a fit.

We say that we do not have it.

You say "...but my phone says that you do."

We say that our eyes say that we do not.

You say that you already paid for it.

We say "you will receive a refund sometime in the next..." Well, I wouldn't keep checking your phone.

You know who does have it?

Amazon.

Amazon has it.

I am not a monster.

I shop local and support small businesses.

But if I need Brita Standard Water Replacement Filters, BPA Free, 2 count, and I need them yesterday, you can bet your ass I am on Amazon, you jackass.

To: Georgia Kay

BEST WISHES FOR CHRISTMAS

AND

THE NEW YEAR

Merry Christmas! 2022 ♡

From Grandy

LOYALTY PROGRAMS

We know most of you do not want to sign up for another rewards program or apply for another credit card. We know, okay?

The questions are annoying. We get it. You are in a hurry and are just trying to leave and pick up some twelve piece chicken strips plus two sides piece-of-shit dinner for your hungry family.

But see....the TPS reports. Our corporate office tracks which and how often each employee asks by how much information they collect from you. We gotta ask.

Kohl's has employees tap dancing down the aisles, serving quiche and taking Amazon returns. (Desperate and pathetic.)

It is competitive.

My husband and I went into a local furniture store for a new nightstand.

(Mine is too small. The older I get, the more pills, potions, fans, and problems I pile on there. Picture **Grey Gardens,** sans cats.) I need a nightstand I could run a burlesque show on.

There were two customers and four employees. The level of service was excruciating. I felt like we were in a sex trafficking situation. But we went with it because we get it.

We knew in his heart the employee didn't have any real empathy for my nightstand situation. He didn't care that I spilled my tea and yelled the 'F word' at bedtime because I was trying to adjust my fan speed by grabbing the remote control in a reckless manner.

He pretended to listen and care and **that** is how it is done.

His eyebrow was missing a strip of hair down the middle. I told Andy I had seen it before on other people and asked if he thought it was a scar or maybe a trend?

He said how was he supposed to know?

That is how intimate our encounter was. We were that close to his face.

Embrace close this holiday season.

Notice eyebrows.

Really get in there.

Share your information gladly and with a giving spirit. And don't be a jackass.

WEAR THE DAMN MASK

Refusing to wear your mask does not make you a constitutional rights activist. It makes you a jackass.

Here's the thing....when you cross the threshold of that establishment, unmasked and ready to fight, the governor of the great state of Texas does not await you. Nor does the CEO of the company.

An hourly employee awaits you.

An hourly employee that has 99 problems that you just pushed to 100.

That person is just trying to make it through their shift so they can go home and eat a frozen pizza and watch Jingle All the Way, in some pathetic attempt to regain some of that holiday spirit.

This will make some people mad.... but I agree with you non-maskers.

I am a stubborn Texas woman that doesn't want a mask or a vaccine.

#BlessYourHeart #ComeAndTakeIt #IAmNotTheOne

Whatever.

But here is the thing....My opinion doesn't matter. My opinion is not more important than an executive order taped to the front of a building. My opinion is not more important than common courtesy.

In fairness, I am also wrong a lot. I have been using a poultry thermometer on pork for years. Andy discovered this recently and asked, "Is a pig a bird?"

I still stood in the kitchen and thought about it for a while.

Obviously, we all have different opinions on the subject, and it is stressful and upsetting.

Let's remember the 19-year-old greeter is stressed and upset as well.

You having a "Karen" stomping fit at the entrance and schooling her on your rights makes her day that much worse.

Write your congressman. Plaster your views on Facebook. Have a mask burning party.

Just don't be a jackass.

I certainly can't forget to mention you jackasses that line up on tax-free weekend to save 8 CENTS ON THE DOLLAR.

Back-to-school wouldn't be complete without a jackass arguing about why headbands aren't included.

Black Friday is a trigger.
I am choosing not to address it.

CHECKBOOKS

You should not be walking around with a checkbook on your person.

Checkbooks belong hidden in desk drawers, not in your hobo knapsack. (See Chapter 1 and please clean out your handbag. I am begging you.)

Customers are sometimes unhappy with the speed in which we process their checks. The lack of speed is due to the infrequency that we accept one. We forget how.

Some companies have discontinued the acceptance of checks. (NOT ALL HEROES WEAR CAPES.)

I shared this fact with an elderly customer recently. She was visibly upset and asked if I knew how many people would be upset if we no longer accepted checks.

I said yes.

Two people would be upset.

She and her neighbor, Helen, that lives two houses down. Helen, who calls the police when a vehicle has been parked on the street longer than 12 minutes.

Helen, the neighbor she waves at when they are both retrieving their mail and reminding each other, "Don't forget to order new checks! Mine have a little kitten holding the flag in his tiny paws! Precious!"

I recently completed a diversity training at work discussing bias. I think old people are slow and annoying. If it is true, is it really a bias? It's just facts.

Remember the scene in **The Godfather** when a guy's hand gets stabbed to the bar with a knife?

That is what I picture when people write checks, but with a pen and the counter.

Lots of payment options!

Don't be a jackass!

Please speak and acknowledge people that speak to you.

Not really retail etiquette as much as plain ol' human being etiquette.

The "greeter" is not a position that people envy. You stand awkwardly at the front of the building and people ignore you as they pass.

If you arrive at Party City, and the greeter says, "Welcome to the party" in a defeated monotone, devoid of joy or energy, just say "Glad to be here!"

He knows it isn't a party. You know it isn't a party. We all know.

If you speak a different language, assume the greeter is saying hello.

Obviously, they are not asking you how often to water perennials.

It is safe to offer a simple "hola" or "bonjour." A smile. A nod.

I am not a big fan of being ignored. I have behaved too aggressively in the past under that assumption only to realize I was in a hearing impaired situation. So be careful.

Prior to my gaining 12 pounds due to Covid lockdown, this handsome young man came into the store and not only returned my greeting but chatted me up.

He was asking a lot of personal questions. I could not understand what was happening because it had been so long.

I asked if he was interviewing me for a newspaper article.

Then he asked if I worked out.

That got a donkey bray.

When he said that, I assumed he was a shoplifter and was about to do a grab-and-run. He was trying to get me vulnerable and catch me off guard.

I thought he was running a long con.

But he left peacefully and told me to tell my husband that he was a lucky man.

(Ha! The man that eats cereal most nights.)

So, be kind.

Say hello back.

Don't be a jackass.

DO SOMETHING ABOUT THEM KIDS

I know we do not leave kids in hot cars. I watch the news.

But now that the weather is cooler, surely it is ok? Right?

If you don't linger and just grab what you need and hurry back out there?

I left the children's retail business in 2020 after half of my life. I had this knot of stress that lived in my neck and shoulder for years.

I tried everything. Physical therapy, chiropractors, medications, massages, etc.... to no avail.

Turns out, it was your kids. Totally pain-free now.

The other day my granddaughter, Madelyn, came into the store and my assistant said, "I have never seen you be nice to a child."

Your kids have licked mirrors, screamed and ran, hid in racks, had fits and talked back, broken crap, touched everything with their filthy grubby little hands, peed and pooped on the floor and thrown up. They have tried on shoes after being held down, only to say that "they hurt" AND they are lying because 100% of kids say that regardless of the style or size of the shoe. Stop falling for it.

They do not behave or listen even when you threaten that you will not buy them the shirt and socks.

Newsflash: They do not care if you buy them the shirt and socks.

Also, they know that you will, in fact, buy them the shirt and socks because you are a liar and never follow through with your threats, even if they spit in your face.

Your children do not need to consume a full meal and hold a lidless red gatorade during the 15 minutes that you are in the building. Surely, they can survive the 15 minutes without sustenance. (I have seen Naked and Afraid.)

At least give them a pork chop. A bone is so much easier to pick up then a stomped bag of Cheetos.

At closing, someone has to sweep and mop all of that crap up.

Don't raise a jackass.

TENDER TIME

Our favorite moment. Selections have been made and you wander up to the cash register.

You look like you are approaching a customs agent in a foreign country.

You have not started digging in your knapsack. You have a confused expression and gingerly put your items on the counter.

Have you purchased things before?

Let us break it down. It is basically a trade. You give me a form of payment and you leave with the items you would like to take to your home. Easy peasy.

We ask for your phone number and of course you don't know it because "You never call yourself!" Indeed. (Willing to bet my weekly wages very few other people call you either.)

The pinpad is upsetting. I get it. Yes, "they are all just so different!"

But, I have to point out...the questions are not SAT questions. They are asking you questions that you probably know.

"Is this amount ok?" That one seems easy enough.

"Credit or Debit?" We understand the difference, don't we? Don't give up!

"Please do not remove your card" or "Please remove your card."

Both make noises that give you tiny hints on how to proceed.

"How would you like your receipt?" Not a lot of choices, really.

Then, if you could just move out of the way for the next jackass, please.

The split tender is always appreciated. A fan favorite.

"Can you put $5 on this card and $4 on this one? I have $6 cash and a roll of quarters. I also have one gold coin, 3 cigarettes, a box of ammo, and a goat."

Selling bags makes things fun. This isn't something Texans really appreciate.

The older people are, the angrier they are. A direct correlation.

Some of my favorites:

"Don't California my Texas!"

Never gets old.

"Pay for a bag? What is in it?"

Well, your items if you buy one.

"WHAT??? People are starving out there. There better be a slice of bread in it!"

"I am never shopping here again."

If only. Literally the least effective threat known to mankind.

"How do you sleep at night?"

Next to a big ass nightstand. Also, with a portable air conditioner, a fan, a sound machine, ear plugs, a leg pillow, and Tylenol PM.

I am not going to mention checks again. I can't. Jackass.

AFTERWORD:

I have spent 40 years in the retail industry and all jokes aside, I have met and formed treasured relationships with so many wonderful people.
I love this business!

I admire and respect all of you for your work ethic, self-control, perseverance, and fortitude. Juggling staffing, payroll, freight, price changes, sales plans, etc... It can be overwhelming. The holiday season definitely amplifies it.

(Restaurant and bar people: You deserve a book, too. I can't write it, but hopefully you can relate to this one. A jackass is a jackass, am I right?)

Christmas is my most favorite time of year! It remains magical to me and I look forward to it all year.
In 40 years, Christmas has not lost its sparkle.

The jackasses have not taken this from me.
So, there is hope for you, my friends.

(This book is a little hateful. I am the opposite of Michelle Obama. When they go low, I go lower.
I just get on my belly and army crawl right under them.)

Thank you for reading this book, and I hope it made you smile and LOL at least once.

Merry Christmas!
Sandy

Happy
Christmas to
You.

GLOSSARY OF TERMS:

JACKASS- A self-centered consumer who has zero regard for the employees serving them or for fellow consumers. They sometimes spit their toothpicks on the floor if shopping after lunch or dinner.

BEEPER- A cashier.

POINT OF SALE- The cash register area, also known as a Cash Wrap.

CHICAGO FIRE- A weekly NBC "program" watched by older people with low viewing expectations.

FORD F150- Trucks driven by white men that live in Texas.

DELIVERING FEEDBACK- Telling your employees crap that they do not want to hear and do not care about because they make $10 an hour.

> (I once gave a well-thought-out and impassioned monologue to an associate that seemed to be listening intently. She stared at me, riveted, and then asked, "Are you wearing a wig?")

COACHING IN THE MOMENT- Telling your employees crap that they do not want to hear and do not care about because they make $10 an hour, immediately, instead of waiting until the next day because you really don't care either and just can't deal with it.

THE DAYS OF OUR LIVES- A long running "story" that dates back to 1965. I haven't seen it since 1986 but could watch it this afternoon and be all caught up.

STEPHEN KING- My favorite author and inspiration. He solidified my lifelong love of reading.

ECOMM- (ecommerce) Commercial transactions conducted on the internet and the demise of brick and mortar.

SIS- Southern term for females. (Can be used in a condescending manner if needed.)

BOPIS- Buy Online Pick Up in Store (Retail workers literally hate this process. Get up and come in and gather your own items, you lazy jackass.)

FIELD- Those of us actually working in stores. Not to be confused with "HQ" (headquarters) people that sit at desks and issue insane directives that are usually not well-thought-out, make little sense, and cause great stress and anguish.

12 PIECE CHICKEN STRIP PIECE-OF-SHIT DINNERS- A drive-thru meal that Moms who do not care about their families pick up after work or yoga.

> (Golden Chick is my personal favorite. I picked up Long John Silvers a lot too, when my kids were young, but am scared to say it because of the shame and harsh judgement.)

TPS REPORTS- An Office Space reference. Watch it.

CHECKS- An archaic form of payment. It is paper. Yes. Paper. I said what I said.

GREETER- A retail worker forced to stand in the front of the business issuing hellos to unreceptive jackasses.

GRAB-AND-RUN- This is when a customer grabs unpaid product and runs out the door. Retail workers stand and watch, sigh, and slowly walk (shoulders slumped) to the office to file an incident report that results in zero resolution.

SHOPLIFTER- A nefarious individual that enters the store with the sole purpose of leaving the store with unpaid product.

Bad ones have big empty purses, wrinkled bags from stores that closed in 1996, are loud and obnoxious, ask stupid questions, and stare at you awkwardly. Good ones come and go and you usually notice the missing product later. Either way, you sigh and walk slowly (shoulders slumped) to the office and file an incident report that results in zero resolution.

At a meeting once, a Regional Director was trying to connect with all the store managers by using humor and cleverness. (It helps to be clever and have a sense of humor when utilizing this technique, btw.) He asked the room in a condescending manner, "Why do you guys get so upset and emotional over theft?"

He seemed genuinely confused. He could not understand it.

I think it would be difficult to understand FROM THE SAFETY OF YOUR VEHICLE WHILE STARING AT YOUR IPHONE.

However, when someone calls you an "ugly red-headed bitch" and spits on your floor, emotions tend to run high.

NAKED AND AFRAID- A TV show that features naked people trying to survive in the wild with few to no supplies.

(I would not make it out of the back of the truck they drop them off in. It is very hot in the wild and climbing out of the truck would burn my nethers.)

ABOUT THE AUTHOR:

Sandy Thornton is a politically incorrect redhead that loves her family, books, and fried chicken.

On a recent vacation, her daughters added up all the books on her Kindle. (Roughly the same dollar amount that is in her 401(k).)

She is the happiest married woman on the planet, thanks to Andy Thornton.

She continues to work in retail, and loves to engage with the occasional jackass.

She remains petty.

Don't be a jackass!

Merry Christmas, Jackass! by Sandy Thornton

Published by Sandy Thornton and Alex Taylor

Cover and Designs by Emily Tomasella

Edited and Managed by Alex Taylor

www.merrychristmasjackass.com

Created and Distributed in The Great State of Texas, USA